Presented To:

Nuadu Tranese Boles

From:

Date:

9/4/2016

Other Books by Pamela K. Dillon

ENCOUNTERS WITH LEADERSHIP: PRODUCING AND PROMOTING HEALTHY LEADERS

Step-by-step instructions and forms to assist in developing true Godly leaders. Co-written by Pastor John W. Dillon.

GIVE HIM THE ASHES

Deep and precious revelation into the process of proper recognition and disposal of the ashes of life.

THANK GOD? FOR POOKIE'NEM

An intricately woven journey through the pathways of life, revealing the various forms of Pookie'nem.

To order books and learn more visit:
WWW.AGAPETIMEMINISTRIES.COM

Agape Time Ministries Inc. - City of Refuge
2280 North Waterford Drive
Florissant, MO 63033-2302

THE
GREATER YES

Answering the Call of God

Written by
Pamela K. Dillon

Staleon Group
Publications
St. Louis, Missouri • Orlando, Florida • 2016

The Greater Yes: Answering the Call of God

Copyright © 2009, 2016 by Pamela K. Dillon.

All rights reserved. No part of this book may be reproduced or transmitted in any form or by any means without written permission from the author.

Second Edition.

ISBN-13: 978-16-827-3765-1
ISBN-10: 16-827-3765-9

Scriptures referenced: The Holy Bible, King James Version. New York: American Bible Society: 1999; Bartleby.com, 2000. New King James Version © 1982 by Thomas Nelson, Inc. All rights reserved. Used by permission.

Merriam-Webster's Collegiate Dictionary (11th ed.). (2005). Springfield, MA: Merriam-Webster.

Staleon Group Publications, PO Box 592203, Orlando, FL 32859-2203.

The Staleon Group Publication logo is a trademark of Staleon Group Publications.

Printed in the United States of America

Dedication

This work is dedicated back to the giver of this gift of writing, Elohim, the Creator. My God in Whom I trust, adore, and love.

I also give my unending love and thanks to my teammate, friend, loyal companion, and biggest fan, my husband John W. Dillon.

I also dedicate the words in these pages to the many men and women in my life who have helped to mold and shape me into the vessel of God I have become. Some have been mentors, friends, pastors, and comrades. I will refrain from naming you all, because I may leave out the most important ones.

To my sons Michael and Alvin Frazier and their families, and Brittany and Stephanie Dillon and their families may the words in these pages inspire you all to greatness. To our ministry son and daughters may the will of the Lord overtake you and you find counsel, direction, and insight in these letters.

Table of Contents

Dedication xii

Foreword 1

Introduction 5

Encounter I: When Your Water Breaks 7

Encounter II: Can You Pray In the Desert? 19

Encounter III: Can You Hear the Father Breathing... 39

Encounter IV: Exchanging Physical Cravings for Spiritual Groaning 47

Encounter V: Picking Up the Mantle 57

Encounter VI: Who Am I? 65

Encounter VII: In His Presence 69

Encounter VIII: Walking With God 73

Closing Prayer 75

Foreword

Pamela Dillon is known as a dynamic speaker who demonstrates the heart of the Father. Pastor Dillon is highly sought after as one who is able to provide critical support to leaders through effective strategies releasing healing and support. Her ministry is marked by prayer and supernatural healings that spontaneously take place in the presence of the Lord.

The Greater Yes is a timely book for the body of Chris, as it provides insight and answers for the believer as they walk out their journey. The Greater Yes reminds us that God still requires a YES in our spirit, and a willing heart and mind to do HIS will. It is a powerful revelation that speaks to the church of the ultimate cost in serving God in every season: a complete surrender, the cry of yes.

The Greater Yes will provoke and stimulate you to give the response that God requires, that brings greater glory in your life.

If you have found yourself frustrated with destiny call and purpose, The Greater Yes will catapult you back on track as it touches the depths and heart cry of God for a right response from creation in every season.

As you read the revelation of the Greater Yes, get ready to have your appetite increased towards God as you cry Yes to

His will and way, bringing pleasure and delight to the Father.

Apostle Ilinda Jackson
The Secret Place Community Church
Oklahoma City, Oklahoma

'For our light affliction, which is but for a moment, worketh for us a far more exceeding and eternal weight of glory' (2 Corinthians 4:17, KJV).

Introduction

When I began to get the inspiration to pen this book this thought came to me. I thought about when a man asks a woman to marry him and how he anxiously awaits for her answer of "yes". The woman responds by saying yes. She is not just saying yes to an elaborate wedding and all the fanfare the day brings for the bride. But this yes means a commitment to a lifetime of friendship, hardship, and relationship. Not just a relationship of cohabiting but one of communing one with another, the good, the bad and the ugly. This is how the female feels as well as the man receiving her. Often when the female says yes - her heart thumps with happiness and the male's thuds with, oh my goodness she said *yes*. This means commitment. This means drama forever. This means I am responsible to her. The yes is supposed to mean, I will adore you for eternity.

Many servants of the Lord called into ministry think and feel that answering their call to preach, teach, or sing the gospel is the ultimate yes and marriage to God. It is only the beginning to personal ministry and a lifelong commitment to repeatedly saying yes to the Lord.

The scripture says to make your calling and your election sure (2 Peter 1:10-11). Why would the word of God say to make it sure? Because God the creator- Elohim, knew there was going to be a greater experience that will take place between your election your calling and you before He returns.

INTRODUCTION

There will be many obstacles in life and ministry that may cause us to second guess ourselves and even to shy away and look back to a more simpler time before we answered the call of ministry for the sake of the Kingdom of God.

Saying yes to any call or vocation placed upon your life is just the beginning of the journey. This statement holds true for the business administrator, to the school teacher, to the pulpit minister.

The Greater Yes is a lifelong commitment to His presence that we might stay in the *yes* mode of doing God's will - God's way with a pure motive and sacrificial determination.

In the Greater Yes I talk seriously, candidly and humorously of the transitions we take in our desire to commitment to a deeper relationship with the Lord. As we walk out, our God given assignments.

Often on these pages God the Father has given me a pure revelation and divine instruction as to what is actually happening to us as we surrender to the call of God on our lives and more importantly the call to rest from our laborers and to serve in His presence as we seek him intimately daily.

ENCOUNTER I

When Your Water Breaks

Most of the time when we hear it said, "My water broke", we allude it to a pregnant woman who is in labor and is now ready to deliver her baby. I had wondered in my spiritual mind what makes me and the people of God cry when we hear the word of God come forth. It might be a personal individual word or the prophetic word preached out over the pulpit to thousands causing the anointing of the word of God to pierce our spiritual womb and cause us to cry which provokes our water to break.

When a pregnant woman makes the announcement," My water broke" This is the time when everyone surrounding this woman gets really serious, gets in a panic, and starts moving very quickly. Everything that is in the woman's way must be moved so that she can get through. She needs to get to a place to deliver. Most of the time the mother to be is well prepared for this inevitable moment in time. Her suitcase is packed and sitting by the door. It is an old wives tale that most mamas are so anticipating this moment that she cleans her house the week before unbeknownst to the fact that the baby is really coming within a week. Mama intuition is what it's called.

Although this explains what happens in the natural to pregnant woman, this process of our water breaking happens to male and female alike when it comes to birthing spiritual babies. Both male and female become very uncomfortable in the body. Naturally, a pregnant female becomes very uncomfortable. None of her regular clothing fits. Some pregnant women feel that everyone is looking at them and noticing the change and noticing the irregular way their clothing is fitting. This dilemma holds true for spiritual parents to be who become very uncomfortable in the present surroundings. For some reason, you no longer seem to fit in a body of believers, that you have always felt comfortable with. Suddenly the atmosphere does not seem like something you have a taste for. You become annoyed with the food you always like. The food you have always liked at times seems to give off a smell that makes you sick.

Cravings

Whether you are male or female there is a time when your water breaks and it is a spiritual baby that must come forth. Like a natural baby, you must get in a place to deliver. This place must be sterile and conducive to delivering a baby safely. It has always puzzled me that when a child of God, male or female, announces that they are pregnant with a spiritual baby- in other words, God has placed ministry in their spirit and called them to a specific work in the kingdom of God. It is amazing how many people act like they did not know the person was pregnant. Many act as if they did not see the signs. The signs are usually seen first in their eating habits. There is an increase and unusual eating habits, such as more times of getting in the word to eat all hours of the morning and night. This behavior is described by more intense times of prayer, fasting and reading the word of God. Many begin to attend more church meetings and seem to soak up every word spoken about God and what He is doing. You can find these pregnant people hanging out in the lobby of the church they will not go home right away. These people are drawn by the hunger and thirst in them to feed the spiritual baby that is kicking on the inside.

The Parents to be are always looking for some place to eat. Sometimes they go to unusual places to eat. These Spiritual parents to be are seen in different camps, i.e. you may see a charismatic in a more catholic service and vice versa. You may see an African-American in an all Caucasian service and vice versa. In essence your taste buds change and you are attempting to feed the craving of your personal ministry. You must know that your spiritual baby will crave the food needed to encourage it to grow and to give it identity. The spiritual baby craves the food that feeds its desire and promotes the advancement. You most likely will be drawn to the people and spiritual feedings which identify with your calling or your specific gift or gifting in the earth. Sometimes you are not even aware of what that means or what the identity of your baby will be. Most of the time spiritual parents to be cannot even explain what is going on inside their spiritual womb.

You must have a balanced diet when pregnant and eat foods that agree with you - because toxic foods will cause you to be sick and have an upset stomach. The problem is sometimes we don't know that the food is bad until we have digested it or after it has set on our stomachs for a while and it begins to sour. Our stomachs can be described as our spiritual womb. The scripture says that out of our belly shall flow rivers of living waters. However, if the water is stagnated in the well it will not come forth pure. Many of us have allowed our wells to become stale and stagnated by the impurities we allow to infiltrate our system. Sometimes the body craves and hungers for things we should not have just because we are hungry to learn, grow and progress.

I read somewhere that sometimes when we overreact - it is simply because we are thirsty. Jesus said, "But whosoever drinketh of the water that I shall give him shall never thirst; but the water that I shall give him shall be in him a well of water springing up into everlasting life" (John 4:14, KJV). Jesus is beckoning us to come commune with him, rather than eating from every table and eating all the time at everyone's house. Not to say that we must not eat out or in other words visit other ministries. The more we commune with Him the more we become spiritually keen and are more sensitive to smell or discernment of bad food before it gets to our mouth so we don't eat it at all. Ask yourself, do you eat food that smells bad and/or looks bad intentionally? No, you do not - not unless you are starving and have not eaten in a long time. Anything looks good.

It is evident in the body of believers that we are eating from tables that we should not. Why? Because the symptoms in the body show we are toxic, upset, and agitated. However, when we have a well-balanced diet we grow and we look healthy. The anointing that we carry is one of lasting change. Have you ever observed a believer who is expectant and eating the right diet, making all the checkups, going to all the meetings needed to keep on track for the set delivery date of their spiritual birth. These believers look exuberant they're glow and appear to be illuminated with the word of God. Those who eat wrong- eat long and go past their due dates. The ministry becomes sluggish and non-productive.

A baby does new things at each period of gestation. Your spiritual baby does the same thing; it kicks, moves and nudges you. Especially when you hear a word or receive food much needed - your baby will kick and exclaim that it is enjoying the impartation of food.

If your baby does not kick every now and then and you feel that you have gone past your delivery date, this is a time you must check yourself, your spirit, and then check your delivery room or in other words the ministry you are a part of. Is this place pure and conducive for delivering a baby. Every natural baby born needs assistance to make its arrival in the earth. Every spiritual baby needs assistance as well. Occasionally there are babies that pop right out with no assistance- however, they too must have assistance. Someone has to cut their cord. Someone has to wash the blood away, so one has to see that the baby is breathing and has all it fingers, toes, and both eyes and ears. Everyone one needs assistance, everyone needs a mentor, everyone needs a spiritual midwife, everyone must have a spiritual parents.

Designated Spiritual Family

'And the Child grew and became strong in spirit, filled with wisdom; and the grace of God was upon Him. His parents went to Jerusalem every year at the Feast of the Passover. And when He was twelve years old, they went up to Jerusalem according to the custom of the feast.

When they had finished the days, as they returned, the Boy Jesus lingered behind in Jerusalem, And Joseph and His mother did not know it; But supposing Him to have been in the company, they went a day's journey, and sought Him among their relatives and acquaintances. So when they did not find Him they returned to Jerusalem, seeking Him. Now so it was that after three days they found Him in the temple, sitting in the midst of the teachers, both listening to them and asking them questions. And all who heard Him were astonished at His understanding and answers. So when they saw Him, they were amazed; and His mother said to Him, "Son, why have You done this to us? Look, Your father and I have sought You anxiously" And He said to them, "Why did you seek Me? Did you not know that I must be about My Father's business?"' (Luke 2:40-49, NKJV).

The Problem with most ministry carriers or spiritual people with a child is that they try to make their baby look just like everyone else's baby. I have often wondered why. Just as natural babies have different parents and designated parents, we must have spiritual parents and God-given parents. The spirit of the Lord actually gives us entire spiritual families and mid wives to assist us with birthing our ministries.

There is a pre-planned birth canal or journey that we all most past through and this canal is individualized. It is a stream and path that we must get in to flow perfectly and successfully to our destination.

Just a Jesus stated, "I have come to do the will of my Father". The ministry in us cries out to do the ministry of the Father. However, we must connect with our spiritual fathers and mothers on the earth to effectively complete the journey.

Each parent has a significant role, our natural birthing parents and our spiritual birthing parents. Many times they can be one in the same. But most likely we will have two separate parents and many midwives and mid-husbands along the way. Our task is to be able to identify when we have connected with our spiritual parents. Natural parents are easy to know because we have grown up with them and known them since birth. We look like them physically, carry their last names and have many of their attributes. We can have their attributes and mannerisms even if we were adopted because we grew up under their care and direction.

Natural Parents

Our natural parents groom us and set us in the direction towards our spiritual parents. They put us in the vicinity and proximity of our spiritual parents. We can be lead to our spiritual parents. Just as Jesus was taken to the Feast of Passover by his parents we are taken to church by our parents or even groomed in a certain way to desire the fellowship of going to temple, synagogue, or church. In my own life at a very early age my parents did not attend church regularly, however, I would hear them speak of God and having a very evident reverence for the Lord by the things they did concerning the Lord. So this desire formed inside my spirit to be curious about church and Jesus. I was taken to church on occasion, I began to love it on my own and desired to get on the church bus or walk to church at a very early age on my own.

The bible says and a child will lead them- as this was true with Jesus's life- it was true with my life as well. My hunger and desire spilled over onto my parents and my mother later became saved, and filled the Holy Spirit, and a very powerful leader in her church later in her life. Mother than became a constant reminder to me the importance of being "filled the holy ghost, living right, acting right, and talking right."

Mama's Words

My mama often gave me this message with power, an outstretched hand pointing toward my heart, and an amplified voice that penetrated my soul and spirit, "Pamela you have to live holy, to be holy, and IF you are holy in, you will be holy out." These words direct my life still today and forever. So in turn my natural parent became a designated spiritual parent as well and the mantel of holiness which she embodied passed to me upon her death.

PREMATURE Delivery

Spiritual Parents experience the joys and the woes of parenthood. One of the most devastating losses is PREMATURE delivery. I describe this as when a spiritual child in which God has placed in your care pushes and pushes until it is delivers itself way before time.

It is painful and most of all unexpected - as a parent, the spirit of the Lord has shown you the time and the season for the spiritual child to be birthed into its own ministry and walk alone. So when it begins to push and kick and burst the walls down so that he or she can be seen by the world without standing in the shadow of the parent. It is very tense and unexpected time.

The baby begins to kick and scream by wanting its way. Not adhering to chastisement. Many times the attitude and characteristics reassemble that of the Jezebel or Abasolam spirit.

It is one that sows discord and forms its own inner circle within the circle. The baby begins to kick and spit up on you in the womb and if you are not careful you will become sick as well. The baby displays the attributes of leadership but in reality it has started wearing big peoples clothes and eating big peoples food and not able to digest it rightfully. So therefore it causes the baby to spit up all over other people and cause them to smell and be tainted by the regurgitated food. As well as making the spiritual covering to sag and look sloppy, because the clothes were on the outside and in public reflect the house in which they were dressed. In other words you make the pastors and spiritual parents in any capacity look as though they dressed you wrong or did not teach you how to dress - mostly by not teaching you the Word. As my mama, Mother Smith, used to say, "don't go out there making me look bad – 'cause I know I taught you better."

With PREMATURE babies they must be put in an incubator and given breathing treatments and be put on oxygen. They are usually placed in a glass incubator for everyone to see- however, they are not fully dressed and it is evident to the whole world that they are not breathing on their own and that they made their entry into the world too soon.

Newborns Make It Hard

Most of the time premature babies are no fault of the mothers only 12% of babies in the United States or 1 in 8 of all births are premature each year. According to Wikipedia- a free informational encyclopedia, there are several known risk factors however, nearly half of all premature births have no cause. So when we look in the CHRISTENDOM and compared the same statics. We could almost say that using the same number and facts. The premature ministries that we have in the body are mostly no fault of the parents but it has derived from the baby having a mind, soul, and spirit of its own. The person with ministry has his or her own will in which they are being led by. Rather than being coached, mentor, persuaded and taught by leadership, some newborns choose to crawl off and get into all kinds of trouble. Because crawling is something you have to be down on your knees to do it is evident that you are low to the ground and the person attempting to help you must either get down where you are and or extend you a hand to reach for. When you are low to the ground it means that you have lost moral boundaries and biblical principles and concepts do not rule your mind. You are led by what feels good to you and seemingly causes you to reach your destination faster. That destination being a seat of authority that is not yet ready for you to obtain. There are no shortcuts to high ranking leadership. The shortcut is to be obedient and you get there smarter but not always faster. Obedience is always better than sacrifice, isn't that what the bible says. Obedience always gets you to your destination on time. To some it seems a long time coming. It is from my experience that I have seen many crawl away and not reach up for the helping hand nor allow for someone to meet them where they are and help them come up to a higher place in God.

The sad fact of the matter is that many newborns assume the position of sitting and standing. When they are unable to maintain either position without weaving, waddling, and eventually falling down. What I mean in saying this is that the newborn person in ministry wants to stand in a place of authority. However, the weight of the responsibility and anointing they are not able to handle. Have you ever witnessed a person who wants the prestige so bad of being in a position of notoriety, that they will forsake anybody and anything to get there. So these perpetrators assume the position and hurt others' lives as they manipulate, and push their way through to the top. However, when they finally get to the seat in the pulpit or the front row seat. This same person finds it is not as easy as they imagined and even boasted to others that they could handle. It is always better to wait your turn. You can use the experiences of others to learn from and you can watch, fight, and pray without feeling any of the real licks.

One time my husband told me that he prayed a silly prayer- and you will agree with me after I tell you. That it is silly. He said that he prayed and asked the Lord to give him the burden of our mentor and overseer in ministry. So he happened to pray this prayer while driving down the highway. So the Lord answered as he so often does when we pray. The weight of this burden gripped my husband heart and mind so heavy that he said, Lord, he exclaimed, Lord get this off me- take it away. This just goes to show that sometimes even when we innocently ask to carry other burdens that it is too much for us to carry. Often times people in leadership cause the burden and or vision in which they carry to seem light and not overwhelming. However, when a person who is not fully equipped to handle that particular burden will buckle under that type of pressure. So needless to say my husband does not pray in the manner. He may pray more wisely by saying Lord equip me to help them carry the Load.

ENCOUNTER II

Can You Pray In The Desert?

We have all had a midnight experience when it was 11:59 on our circumstances of life. We needed Jesus to show up, quick and in a hurry. There are times when it seems as though 11:59 last for months, even years. It seems as though Jesus is taking his time to deliver us.

Psalms 23 is a favorite scripture for many and one of my personal favorites as well. I begin to really look at that scripture and listen to revelation that was coming right off the pages in which I seemed to have missed for so many years, especially when I find myself at 11:59 moment.

Psalms 23 reads:
'The Lord is my shepherd; I shall not want. He maketh me to lie down in green pastures: he leadeth me beside the still waters. He restoreth my soul: he leadeth me in the paths of righteousness for his name's sake. Yea, though I walk through the valley of the shadow of death, I will fear no evil: for thou art with me; thy rod and thy staff they comfort me. Thou preparest a table before me in the presence of mine enemies: thou anointest my head with oil; my cup Runneth over. Surely goodness and mercy shall follow me all the days of my life: and I will dwell in the house of the Lord forever.' (Psalms 23, KJV).

Still Waters

As I begin to search deeper into this verse, I know that the Lord is my shepherd - Jehovah- Ropha - he is guides the way, he leads and directs the activity and performance of my life. He restoreth my soul- he replenishes-brings my soul back to its original state. The next portion is what I have seemed to have missed or skipped right over this portion of text, or perhaps- I comprehended it wrong. He (the Lord) leadeth me beside the still waters. The word still is what missed. Still means motionless or without motion, a state of calm or quietness, making no sound or not moving. So in essence the Lord is saying to us that he will lead us to a place in time where there is no motion. There will be no activity. The Lord will accompany us to a place in our lives where we must wait for him. It will seem to be a place in our lives where nothing is happening. It seems this way because it is true there is not activity. There are no ministry engagements, or assignments. We are in a place of stillness that appears non-productive. If we are not careful at this point in life we will jump out of our stream into another stream because it is moving. What am I saying here you will start to feel lead to start doing another work like making albums or writing books, or selling real estate. Not to say that the Lord does not want you to be in these streams of life. But we sometimes jump out of one flow into another that seems more lucrative before our season of walking in these gifts. All because of nonproduction. So we then exhaust ourselves with accomplishment. When all the time the spirit of the Lord is calling us to a place of stillness. We all know that we hear him best in the stillness. At lot of times God says nothing and that is when he is saying the most. Sometimes no talking is a time of impartation and we have perceived it as non-activity. It seems as though we are marching in time and not going forward. It seems as though you are standing still-because you are in the physical.

You are in a place which some call a dry place - a desert place. Some call it a winter or night season. I call it a season of still waters. It is the making place of every true man and woman of God. The reason why it can be described as still is because before this time-you were moving.

You were moving in ministry, you had engagements, you were active in the public eye. Or whatever your discipline or career you were actively pursuing. Whether you are a singer, author, musician, pastor, prophet, priest, talk show host or president of the United States of America everyone hits a dry season a still time.

Many have viewed this time a unfruitful and detrimental to their livelihood. In essence this is the season you find out whether you can pray in the desert. Still waters are a place where the Lord is with you, but he may not be speaking very much. Perhaps this is what makes it such a difficult place because although you feel his presence, you don't hear his voice for direction. You hear his voice but it does not tell you to do anything. You may see his face - but not feel his hand. The Lord basically tells you that he loves you and that he will never leave you nor forsake you. I have found from experience this seems to be an annoying place if I can be truthful because, you want to do something, you want to hear some directives, and instructions on where to go and what to do, and whom to do it with. Let's face it - we want something to be happening all the time. You feel the comfort and the outstretched hand of the spirit of the Lord but it is not enough. How could we be so bold to think this but we do. Why, because we feel that actions and motion describes God's love rather than his presence.

This awkward season is where many make bad choices and have to make up for lost time and regroup from bad decisions made. You know like marrying the wrong man or woman. Or like moving from the church the Lord has planted you in. You know like stepping out before your hear the direction of the Lord into fulltime ministry. You know all the things we do during the stillness of the night season. Most of the times we make these hasty decisions after being in a place of motionlessness - nothing happening - that fulfills our senses.

Let's talk about the positive of the Stillness of the water. We know that when water is mentioned - spiritually it means the Holy Spirit - most of the time. So for the Holy Spirit to be motionless or without movement would suggest that time has stopped. However, we know that the Holy Spirit is active, and alive. We know that it was the Holy Spirit that moved upon the deep (in Genesis 1: 2) and the Spirit of God moved upon the face of the waters. Anytime the Holy Spirit or Spirit of God moves upon something, it creates. Whatever is null or void comes into formation. The voice of the Lord is still and quite-although it clamors and stirs up a ruckus when he comes in to create. I asked myself how could something be still and loud at the same time. The Holy Spirit answered the question by taking me to the scripture in Ezekiel 4.

'And, behold, the glory of the God of Israel came from the way of the east: and his voice was like a noise of many waters: and the earth shined with his glory.' (Ezekiel 43:2, KJV).

The Stillness of God's voice, reminds me of when you are getting ready to attempt something that makes you very nervous. On the inside you feel as though you are going to explode- the palms of your hands may become wet. You can feel the blood rushing to your face, you feel very shaky, however, most people looking upon you are unaware that you have just experienced several different sets of emotions, fear, joy, regret, happiness, and determination. When you tell someone I was so nervous- most will say I could not tell it did not appear that you were afraid or nervous at all. The anointing of the Lord came upon you and shined in your earth. In other words we are made of dirt- the earth and the spirit of the Lord comes upon us to shine in the things we accomplish for the Lord.

The stillness of the God the Father's voice reminds me of this because nobody can usually see him moving unless that have a kin sense of discernment or know you very well. In the stillness and quietness - usually explosive events are taking place in the spiritual world, however, to the natural eye it appears calm and inactive.

A Place in Creation

Could it be that God takes us to a place in creation and eternity that is incomprehensible to our natural minds? Could it be that the spirit of the Lord takes us to a place of seemingly stillness to impart the voice of many waters? He moves systematically and orchestrates every move, that everything is set in place and in time for the inhabitants or those who will occupy the space he has created.

In other words when God has brought you into a place of stillness he is birthing something in you and setting an atmosphere for it to grow and reproduce. At this time you are sensitive to light and darkness, you are sensitive to sound, and everything that surrounds you. So the Lord God protects you during this stage and places you in a realm of safety - which appears to you as a place of silence. When, in essence, it is a place of developing and equipping. It is a place where you settle yourself in the things of God. This is a place of securing yourself with a true foundation. It is a place in eternity.

Everyone does not master this particular place because it seems so senseless and nonproductive. In life you will visit this place for each new realm of ministry. This not only holds true for people in ministry, but this is evident even in the secular world or with people in general, you will find that every gifted person will pull back for a season in their careers. So that they may come out with something fresh, something new. Corporations do this, ad agencies, musicians, etc. Everyone has a place where creativity must be born and it is usually birth in the place of stillness.

Out of Your Belly

Jesus said that the Holy Spirit is like well of water that springs up: 'But whosoever drinketh of the water that I shall give him shall never thirst; but the water that I shall give him shall be in him a well of water springing up into everlasting life.' (John 4:14, KJV)

Why is it that when people of God touch your belly to stir up the gift of God in you, which is the Holy Spirit or living waters. If feels as though your belly is on fire- moving- alive. It feels ignited. However, many of miss our opportunities of impartation. We swap time in God's presence for outside activities and interaction with other sources. Sometimes the sources appear to be something good and even God like- but they are in essence time stealers and belly flops.

Look what God speaks to his people in Jeremiah:

'Hath a nation changed their gods, which are yet no gods? But my people have changed their glory for that which doth not profit; Be astonished, O ye heavens, at this, and be horribly afraid, be ye very desolate, saith the Lord. For my people have committed two evils; they have forsaken me the fountain of living waters, and hewed them out cisterns, broken cisterns, that can hold no water.'(Jeremiah 2:11-13, KJV).

Verse thirteen caught my attention- God says that his people have committed two evils: "They have forsaken me- the fountain of living waters, and hewed out cisterns, broken cistern, that can hold no water." God is saying to us that we have fortified out time with him who is the life giver and we have hewed or made, created our own anointing. Oh my. We have forsaken the Father by forgetting about him by swapping intimacy with productivity. So we go about doing the work of the ministry and denying the power thereof. So in other words we are often times running on empty. We miss our times of impartation for a ministry engagement. Impartation occurs when the fountain of living waters flow and surge through our soul man and spirit man. Living waters are purifying and divide the soul from the spirit. The purification also brings the soul and spirit back together as one. Living waters cause us to operate out of pure motive. Those who fail to receive this impartation don't last long and/or their assignments in the earth become superficial or selfness.

Pure water brings clear assignments, although it may seem cloudy at the time of impartation as you flow in the things of God-tasks given by God are delivered and administered with effectiveness and lives are changed forever. You can usually tell the difference between someone who has waited on their ministering in the presence of the Lord before coming before people, to speak, pray, or sing. The anointing is heavy, the anointing is true, and the anointing is real and life changing. A stirring comes in your soul when they hit the stage or come in your presence at any time. The gift coming from them reaches right into your spirit and pulls out assignment, pulls out a baby. It causes your vision to leap within you. A freshness comes- the word says that times of refreshing comes from the presence of the Lord. You only obtain this freshness by becoming a recipient of the fountain of living waters.

Market Place Anointing

Listen, let me tell you, there are people called of God that are not in the pulpit only. They are business men and women, who have been strategically placed in the marketplace for our benefit. So don't think I am only talking to people called to the church. The church is where you take it. I have experienced my whole world change by a 5th grade teacher whose name was Ima Pigg, really that was my 5th grade English teacher's name. Mrs. Pigg never made any indication whether she was a Christian or not. All I know is that when she came into my presence a stirring would come in my spirit. At the time I did not know what it was. Mrs. Pigg gave a class assignment that we were to write a 500 word essay. That we could choose any topic we liked Thus is when the gift began. Mrs. Pigg stirred up the writer's gift in me. When the class turned in their papers- she chose 5 papers to read and mine was one of them- I used the word befriend in my paper that is all I can remember after- all these years- and she said Pamela where did you learn that word. I stated it just came to me as I was writing. What in essence had happened unbeknownst to me was I had allowed myself to be filled by the fountain of living waters- which enables and gives the ability that you do not possess on your own. Mrs. Pigg was so thrilled with my paper and of course I received an A+ for my work. Mrs. Pigg was a pure soul placed in the marketplace as a 5th grade English teacher- who encouraged me at a very throughout and delicate age to become a writer. She stated I had the gift. And whatever Mrs. Pigg carried in her belly would always stir me up. Don't underestimate the marketplace encounter because they may be the very person having the anointing and ability to stir you up.

A Dry Place

Most anytime we hear the word desert we think three words: Dry, Hot, and Dusty. The big DHD, that's what I will label it throughout the rest of this writing. DHD has come so often in my own life that I have decided to take out DHD insurance. This insurance is that which causes me to run after the Rose of Sharon which is a lily that springs up in a desert. Yes Jesus is called the Rose of Sharon and this is our refuge for DHD. I should describe what DHD means dry meaning nothing happening, hot because of the passion {my gift} burning within and dusty- because it's just sitting there on the shelf not being used at this particular time.

'I am the Rose of Sharon, and the Lily of the Valleys.' (Solomon 2:1, KJV).

I have often wondered how we get to a desert situation in our lives when we have just been in a place of flowing events and prosperity. Maybe I should describe what a desert situation looks and feels like just in case there is someone who may not be following me at this point and/or have never experienced a DHD. DHD can happen at the most unexpected times and at expected times as well. However, my personal DHD affliction has come when I least expected. For instance, ministry seemingly is going well, there is a great anointing upon me and there are people, money, and assignments. In other words I was dressed up with someplace to go and people to talk too. However, with some warning by the Holy Spirit in prayer I could sense the dry winds approaching, but there was nothing I could do about the contrary winds but pray. These contrary winds were inevitable because there is a place in created time that I must pass through in order to be conformed and transformed into my preordained purpose.

Moses' DHD Experience

'And the child grew, and she brought him unto Pharaoh's daughter, and he became her son. And she called his name Moses: and she said, Because I drew him out of the water.' (Exodus 2:10, KJV).

Moses a servant of God began life in the flow of a river. He was born and placed in the waters of life. God gave him a life that he could have only received by being placed in the water and be drawn from the water. What waters (place) has God put you in which you must be drawn out lives from the well of waters in which He has placed us. We must reach inside our spirit man and draw out the gift of life that the Father God has already placed within us. Once we are drawn out we must be set on dry ground. Much like Moses we live a life of goodness, happiness, and abundance for a period of time until the waters within meaning ministry wells up to boiling passion and we than act out the gift that has always been in us sense we were drawn from the waters, the spirit womb. Do you recognize your "Moses waters"?

When ministry wells up we most often slay the enemy by saying yes to the Lord. Our first sincere yes to the will of the Lord sparks the flow of living waters and thus slays the enemy. However, it will cause us to enter into our next DHD season. Like Moses, we just answered our calling, whether we know it or not. The very act that we acted on the passion within us activated the anointing. So this is how we find ourselves in the desert. It's all necessary, however, hot it may feel.

One Night in the Desert

There is one promise of Jesus, the Anointed One, I desperately desired to rest in during a panicky season is, "I will never leave you nor forsake you." One January night, during one of me and my husband's January fasts, it was 3:00 a.m. and I could not sleep at all. After much twisting and turning, clicking thru the stations on tv and listening to all the passionate ministers on TBN, I came to realize that the Father was calling me to prayer. My prayer room is down the hall from my bedroom, so I got up went in, where there is always a tape or bible on CD playing.

As soon as I put my prayer shawl on my head and wrapped it around me, the presence of the Lord dropped heavily. The presence dropped so heavily that I sat right down on my prayer bench in front of my home made altar. As I sat down, I was immediately caught up into the spirit and I saw myself on a boat out in the middle of the sea, I began to row the boat in until I reached shore, when I got to shore it was desert sand, I got out of the boat, as I walked it was though my feet were heavy and I dug each footstep into the sand, I actually stepped into a footstep that had already been placed there previously by someone else, I looked up and there was a tall rock, a cleft with a point which came out in the front. On top of the mountain stood a presence, it was Jesus himself and his arms were outstretched, I began to weep as I looked upon Jesus, I was so moved within myself that I assume I was going to look away and I heard the Holy Spirit say - watch this like a video. I continued to watch, and Jesus continued to beckon me to come unto him. Then I heard the Holy Spirit say, You know that things happen first in the natural than in the spiritual. Recently within the past 6 months my earthly father has been calling me on the phone a lot, it used to be that I always called him to check and see how he was. You know it is a child's duty to call his parent and check on them. But the tables had been turned and my father had been beating me to the punch and calling me maybe once or twice a week. And not only was he calling me but he wanted to get all of his children together for a family reunion. What you must know is that I have five brothers and two sisters, a total of eight of us and my father has been calling us all in different areas of the country: Texas, Oklahoma, and St. Louis. He was working on getting us together for a reunion, well he chose to have the reunion on our deceased mother's birthday. The Holy Spirit began to say to me, "as your father on earth has began to call you, I, your heavenly Father am calling you." You see it is a much greater reward of fellowship when the Father began to call you, when the Father begins to summon you to prayer, he is about to give you something, he is about to impart some great inheritance, some spiritual truth. How awesome I thought this revelation was.

My friend, Carol McDonnell, who incidentally is a proof writer for this work, read through the pages of this book to make sure I had crossed all my t's and dotted my i's. This particular chapter she stated, ministered to her as she read its pages and began to reminisce and feel the wind of the spirit bringing a remembrance to a particular event in her own life with her earthly Father. I asked Carol if I could share this experience with you the reader. As I felt it would be life changing to many and help many to identify defining moments in your life.

Carol began to reminisce on a desert and wilderness time in her life when things were the worst. Her earthly Father had written a letter to her. It was Psalms 121- it read, "from whence does my help come from? It comes from the Lord, who made heaven and earth." Her earthly father had wrote out the entire Psalm. He said that he was praying for Carol. God gave it to her father, just for her. Carol states that this was the first time her earthly father washed her with the water of the Word of God. It helped me to overcome and press into the love of God. This event birthed Carol into the next phase of her life, she exclaims.

Sit By The Well

'Now when Pharaoh heard this thing, he sought to slay Moses. But Moses fled from the face of Pharaoh, and dwelt in the land of Midian: and he sat down by a well.' (Exodus 2:15, KJV)

I like this so much, that Moses sat by the well. Many may say that he sat down because he had to and because he was tired and thirsty. I want to believe that this is symbolic and prophetic that Moses would sit down. He could have drew from the well, replenished himself and kept going. But he chose to sat down and wait for a moment. In the days of Moses wells were often outside towns or villages. The wells were known to be landmarks and meeting places.

Often times when we are in the desert or DHD, we want to get replenished quickly, we want to go to a place of refreshing, receive a life changing word, feel the presence of the Lord soothing our dry spirits and then we are ready to get up from the well and run to the next event or go for the next assignment. Many times the spirit of the Lord would like for us to sit and wait for the 7 daughters. Once again this is prophetic that he would send seven daughters. We know that seven means completion. When we are led to the DHD place it does not mean that life is over- it means life is beginning on a new level on a new plain. How many times can we say that we have missed the seven daughters of completion because we got up and wanted to do an activity rather than rest in the presence of the Lord.

The Seven Daughters of Completion

There is always revelation within revelation upon revelation in the word of God. That is why we can read the entire bible a thousand times over and always retrieve a more deeper meaning of what the spirit of the Lord has said and is saying to us.

Inheritance

'Now the priest of Midian had seven daughters: and they came and drew water, and filled the troughs to water their father's flock.' (Exodus 2:16, KJV).

I began to talk with my husband, Pastor John Dillon, about some of the history of Jethro and his Hebraic background, because he is so well learned and avid studier of the Torah and Jewish perspective. He began to share with me the reason why the daughters of Jethro were even drawing water from the well considering that the custom was for the sons or males to administer this task of herding sheep. However, Jethro had no sons. Earlier Jethro had abandoned and denounced his worship to pagan gods. So he had been outcast by his kinsmen. Normally if you had no sons, the sons of your tribe and/or kinsmen would help tend to sheep.

It is awesome that Moses would be greeted by seven females or seven daughters. I said to Lord this has to mean something and of course the Holy Spirit answered me back. He replied that these represent the seven daughters of completion. We know that there are seven spirits before the throne of God.

Those seven spirits are the being or character of Christ:

1. The Spirit of the Lord resting upon
2. The Spirit of Wisdom
3. The Spirit of Understanding
4. The Spirit of Counsel
5. The Spirit of Might
6. The Spirit of Knowledge
7. The Spirit of Fear of the Lord

'And there shall come forth a rod out of the stem of Jesse, and a Branch shall grow out of his roots: And the spirit of the Lord shall rest upon him, the spirit of wisdom and understanding, the spirit of counsel and might, the spirit of knowledge and of the fear of the Lord;' (Isaiah 11:1-2, KJV)

We also know that most often in the bible when a woman is mentioned the spirit of the Lord is alluding to the church. So with us knowing that God is most often talking to us about a state or condition we are in as the body of Christ. So if He talks to us about any woman whether she is given a name or not. One must stop and ask the Holy Spirit, what are you really saying? What is the revelation of the woman or the condition we the church or me a bride may be in.

The seven daughters are talked about in a twofold way describing the bride and the bridegroom simultaneously. The attributes of Christ are what the bride is to obtain. As the church we are to mature in the likeness of Christ. If we are to ascend with him when he returns we must be glorified and adorned in the clothes in which he has prepared. These clothes are not garments made of thread. These are garments made from his attributes; garments sewn by his spirit and woven in his love. Each stitch is made from a place in time when you grew in a single attribute. A place when we really began to trust and rest in the spirit of the Lord, a place when we really settled our hearts and minds in his wisdom and made decision based on the wisdom of the Lord. Our lives were led by the counsel of the Lord and with divine understanding, we operated in the might of the Lord and ministered from revelation knowledge from the throne as we worshiped in the reverential fear of the Lord. Oh how awesome that we could reach layer upon layer of this type of anointing experience after experience, testimony after testimony, trial after trial. Glory to the Father.

Each daughter represents an attribute that God desires for us to mature and master before going to the next level in life. Just imagine how much depth our lives and ministry would have if we waited and matured in the Lord resting upon us, his wisdom, understanding, counsel, might, knowledge and fear of the Lord. How awesome we would be if perhaps at every DHD scene in our lives we perfected the seven Spirits of the Lord before proceeding to the next phase. You can never outgrow these, nor master them thoroughly. The reason being each level of life brings on a more skilled way of handling that particular situation. And what we knew on yesterday is of value but there is nothing like having a more sharpened weapon of warfare to deal with daily situations personal and ministry.

As Pastor John and I visited, he brought so much confirmation as to what the Holy Spirit was speaking to me regarding the seven daughters. Pastor John stated, "is it not awesome that the Jethro would give Moses a choice of the seven daughters and Moses choose Ziporrah (Tzipporah in Hebrew)?" Ziporrah was the oldest; she was also the shepherd over all of her sisters, as well as the fighter and had the most wisdom, and understanding. Ziporrah was the daughter with the most passion. Pastor John continued on to say, that she was the woman to help usher and birth Moses into the man God had called him to be. We found that Zipporah's name means *small bird*. I thought- how awesome is that- A woman who could soar above the earth.

This is exactly God's character, he will always give us a choose, even in the desert, and we can choose the more weighty route of maturity or we can take a lesser way which will eventually get us to our destination, but why take the low road when you can take the high road and learn much more in a less amount of time and possess a more weightier anointing.

Making a decision to sit at the well and allow the Spirit of the Lord to mature us through mentor ship, and on the job training is much more lucrative than going it alone and running on empty. So sit by the well the next time you encounter DHD and many times in between.

ENCOUNTER III

Can Hear The Father Breathing?

This Carousel Time

The Carousel goes round and round up and down, round and round. Does that sound like life? There are times when we feel at the top of our game in accomplishing the assignments the Lord has put into our hands. Then there are times when it appears that we are going around in a big circle never going forward, never seeing a new day, never seeing the end of the road. I call this Carousel Time. It seems as though life is passing us by and we are on the merry go round as we used to call it when I was growing up. Bystanders looked on as we go round and round. We would ride the merry go round for a while. It would always be kids standing by waiting to leap on to the merry go round when it slowed down enough, because it looked so fun. Just as there were some who wanted to jump on when it slowed down. At the same time, there were ones who wanted to jump off because they were tired of going around and beginning to get sick. Sometimes others want to get off because they were tired of doing that particular activity and wanted to go on to something else. It was fun to go around on the merry go round when everybody was cheering you on, and laughing with you. But just as soon as the clapping, laughing, and jeering turned into ridicule it was not so fun, and I wanted to get off the merry go round.

Isn't that funny, how the same merry go around that you were having fun go round and round with your friends, suddenly becomes a not so fun experience, and everyone is saying how long are you going to stay on there, stupid, going around and around? It has always puzzled me that the same merry go round that I am attempting to dismantle, someone else wants to get aboard. I have come to the conclusion that carousel time is a time to see if I can hear the voice of anyone else speaking besides my friends, and my own voice which seems very loud.

I used this metaphor to describe how we receive an inspiration to start a work of any kind for the Kingdom of God. Many people who get on with you to ride in the beginning. It is all fun and everyone is excited and assisting you. You have those who do not really help you but they cheer you on and encourage and, give you a push every now and again. However, after a while if circumstances don't change and those walking along side you don't see a advancement or a noticeable accomplishment that meets their standards. These same carousel riders will jump off the carousel and leave you riding by yourself. At the same time they will go get involved with another activity or organization and watch you from the sidelines of another man's vision where they measure you circular movement as failure. Mostly because the carousel riders have went on to a more established work which does not require as much sacrifice. Oh how harsh this sounds but how true it is. Almost every mentor I have ever had has told me of their carousel observation and the skill they now walk in because of this encounter.

'And the Lord God formed man of the dust of the ground, and breathed into his nostrils the breath of life; and man became a living soul.' (Genesis 2:7, KJV).

God is the Creator and Elohim is his Hebrew name. Webster describes create as to bring into being, cause to exist, make, or produce. God created man from the earth or dust of the ground and he then blew hard or puffed into man a divine inspiration or intellect. Strongs concordance describes this act as the two Hebrew words na`pahach and n'shamah. Na`phach means to blow hard or puff and N'shmah meaning divine inspiration and intellect. God breathed into us his life and creative power. As the Lord began to give me insight and a fresh revelation of our beginnings. I began to understand that in order for me to succeed in life. I would need to refer back many times to the life giving inspiration which was given to me from eternity past which is the beginning. God created the human spirit and the human being to be led by the divine inspiration which lives in us. Ephesians 3:20 calls this divine inspiration, the power that works in us.

There are many times in life that I have been on the merry go round. The merry go around that I am referring to in particular is ministry. I knew and now know that God had given me and awesome assignment to complete for Him in the earth. However, the ministry seemed to not be going forward but instead standing still and sometimes appearing to go backwards. When I speak of ministry, I am not just talking about the pastor of a church or someone who is called to work in any aspect of the church. Merriam-Webster describes ministry as the office, duties and functions of a minister.

II Corinthians 3:6 says, "Who also hath made us able ministers of the new testament; not of the letter, but of the spirit: for the letter killeth, but the spirit giveth life." (II Corinthians 3:6, KJV). Jesus gave us all the qualifications to become ministers once we received the Baptism of the Holy Spirit, which he charged the disciples in Acts 1:8 to "wait unto they received power and the Holy Ghost had come upon them." At that point after receiving the power of the Holy Spirit the disciples of Acts and the disciples of the 21st century meaning you and me are able to minister and be called ministers in whatever capacity we work and live. So to minister does not need a certificate or license. Nor does it need a ministry name but rather so the acceptance of the call of God to do the work.

The merry go around experience can seem like carousel time whether you are trying to start a business or start a new career in which God has called you to and placed you in to be a light before men. I took the sidebar to explain ministry to relate to those of you reading this book who may assume that I am just talking to those called to the fore front of ministry or a pulpit. Such as being called a pastor, prophet, apostle, evangelist, or teacher. I am talking to anyone that has been born again. Whether you realize it or not Father God has called you a minister.

Now getting back to the merry go round experience and feeling that I am going nowhere fast. This situation from personal experience is one of embarrassment and feeling of failure and lack of confidence. Like I said earlier, everyone is watching you in the assignment God has given you. Everyone's ministry is flourishing and it seems as though you have great victories here and there but they never amount to great impact that man can actually see from a distance. What I mean in saying this is that many victories are won when someone's life is changed and you have personally caused someone entire life to be transformed through the Holy Spirit- A soul winner. This is a life by life account of different people at different times and no one is really able to see all these people lined up at once. And say to you, oh my, you have done a great work. So in other words you have no particular place to put them and no place for them to gather, but you are still in ministry.

The sad part about this situation is that God is pleased but you are not. God sees these transformations as divine exploits of his goodness and we see it as passing ships on our way to destiny. Christendom has come to the conclusion that you are on a merry go around, not going anywhere if you do not have multi-million dollar buildings or million dollar product sales. All this is fine and wonderful. But this is not the summation of a man or woman. This is not the measuring stick for a great ministry. God has ordained a calling for each man and woman he blew breath into and none of us look the same. Everything God made he said, and this is "good" Meaning this is my presence, this is my expression in the earth. Your expression of who God is in the earth, maybe counseling youth in an urban community. However, your name may never be in lights or an announcement made across the nation. Without you delivering your God breathed expression in the community man would be lost. The measure of man becomes the depth of how well he can hear God breathing and express what is heard in the ears of mankind.

It has been said many times despise not humble beginnings and this is a word of wisdom we must not only consider but we must live by. I say this because humble beginnings take on the characteristics of carousel time. At the beginning of any new endeavor we undergo a tremendous amount of pressure to succeed and get results. The results cause us to measure our anointing based on stuff and things. God never gave us the anointing just to get stuff and things. God did give us the anointing to overcome. Many times in life and in ministry we must overcome and remain an over comer. I John 5:4-5 states, 'For whatsoever is born of God overcometh the world: and this is the victory that overcometh the world, even our faith. Who is he that overcometh the world, but he that believeth that Jesus is the Son of God?' (I John 5:4-5, KJV).

The word of God says that we have overcome the world even our faith. I like how the scriptures says, *anything* that is born of God. This tells us as believers that anything birthed in us by God will overcome. Whatever purpose God has birthed in you, it will live and not die, it shall succeed and overcome the world. Encounters with life's circumstances cause us to take carousel time as rejection and defeat. Carousel time is the time we should step back and see if we can hear the Father breathing.

As I said earlier God breathed or blew N'shamah into our earth bodies. We have to always listen to the Father breathing inside of us. There are times when I close my eyes and settle my mind and spirit. I began to listen to the Father breathing in me and through me. The wind of His spirit is sweet yet strong and mighty. I can hear the spirit breathing life and breathing excellence in my soul. My very being begins to line up with the wind that is within me. I cannot object to the power of the wind of the breath that consumes me when I submit to the sound of the breath. The breath begins to whisper to me" I will never leave you nor forsake you." The breath encourages me. The breath says to me, will you thirst after righteousness? The breath inspires me to remain in right standing. The breath begins to bring me into a revelation of who He is in a greater way. As I listen to the Father Breathing I began to see my own self clearer. I began to not be discouraged and began to see things in a different realm of existence. When the Father breathes the air becomes lighter and the burdens of the assignment become yoke easy. I began to yoke up with the Holy Spirit. I yoke up with eternity past which is my beginning. I find myself running toward my expected end and it is in eyes view. I can see all things when I stand in the place of hearing the Father breath. I love the breath of the Father because it is fresh, and the intellect of his character cannot be compared with anything else in the earth.

Come and hear the Father breathing in your life. Whatever challenges you face in life, in ministry, personal, or corporate. Come and hear what the Father has to say about it. Don't be discouraged by carousel time. Take carousel time as an opportunity to sit and commune with the Lord. Let carousel time not consume you or detour you from reaching your goal. Instead let carousel time be a place of reconciliation with the Father's purpose in your heart to connect with the breath of God. This is the key to accomplishment in life. The key to success is the breath of God. Many times people have tried to feel the breath because they have confused the wind with moving on the outside when it is a wind that moves on the inside of you- the power of God. So don't wait for the outside breath to move on the things of God. Long for the Inside Breath that drives the passion with you. But purpose to hear the breath of God in you, which will stir up the gift of God to execute any assignment given by the King of Kings and Lord of Lords.

ENCOUNTER IV

Exchanging a Physical Craving for a Spiritual Groaning

'And seeing the multitudes, he went up into a mountain: and when he was set, his disciples came unto him: And he opened his mouth, and taught them, saying, blessed are the poor in spirit: for theirs is the kingdom of heaven. Blessed are they that mourn: for they shall be comforted. Blessed are the meek: for they shall inherit the earth. Blessed are they which do hunger and thirst after righteousness: for they shall be filled. Blessed are the merciful: for they shall obtain mercy. Blessed are the pure in heart: for they shall see God. Blessed are the peacemakers: for they shall be called the children of God. Blessed are they which are persecuted for righteousness' sake: for theirs is the kingdom of heaven. Blessed are ye, when men shall revile you, and persecute you, and shall say all manner of evil against you falsely, for my sake. Rejoice, and be exceeding glad: for great is your reward in heaven: for so persecuted they the prophets which were before you. Ye are the salt of the earth: but if the salt have lost his savior, wherewith shall it be salted? it is thenceforth good for nothing, but to be cast out, and to be trodden under foot of men. Ye are the light of the world. A city that is set on an hill cannot be hid. Neither do men light a candle, and put it under a bushel, but on a candlestick; and it giveth light unto all that are in the house. Let your light so shine before men, that they may see your good works, and glorify your Father which is in heaven.' (Matthew 5: 1-16, KJV).

Talley Space

Jesus looked out and saw the multitude of people waiting upon the anointing, waiting to receive the word of the Lord, waiting to receive a miracle. Although these same people who are in waiting to receive from him they had issues and ought against Him as King of Kings. What am I saying? Everyone sitting in a place and wanting to receive your gift does not always want you, the person, they want the gift. Many people in society want what you have to offer, however, if you could drop the goods off at the door and keep step-in. This would be just fine with the people. A lot of times people do not want to connect with you as an individual and form a relationship. Which many did in Jesus's day, many we must say wanted only to connect with the personality of who Jesus was and what he could do for them. Most were unaware that forming a relationship with him was the key to lasting transformation. I love that Jesus never let this stand in his way of delivering the goods or in other words letting the Father breath on the people, giving the people the blessing of the Lord.

I love that Jesus was always a mentor to the disciples. He took every opportunity to teach a lesson right in the midst of the situation. So he looked down and saw the multitudes and he took the disciples or his students off to the side and said look let me show you something. How many ministers do we know would see the crowd waiting and jeering waiting for them to mount the stage, but instead they retreat to the office or dressing room and say, "send my staff or leadership team in I have something to show you at this moment." No that many, it is sad to say. Most want to seize the moment of the waiting crowd and teach the lesson after.

I know that there are many lessons and there are many revelations which can be obtained from Matthew 5 and the beatitudes as they have been so wonderfully named. I don't claim to have the only interpretation. I must share the most eye opening and weight lifting revelation I received from Matthew 5:8 many years ago, that has help me be a mature Christian and weightless in my endeavors to please the Lord and be in his service.

Matthew 5:8 reads, "Blessed are the pure in heart for they shall see God." I pondered on the verse and begin to hear the breath of God in the word. The pure in heart - The pure in heart. What could this possibly mean? I thought Purity only meant that something is clean. But the Merriam-Webster Dictionary defines the word *pure* as:

1. Unmixed with any other matter.
2. Free from taint.
3. Free from what vitiates, weakens, or pollutes.
4. Free from moral fault.

Oh my goodness, so what was the Lord Jesus saying to us, his disciples? He was saying that we needed to keep our heart and minds unmixed with any other matters. The cares of this world and free from the issues of life that taint our spirits. We as servants have to keep clear of toxins that pollute our heart and mind to become innocent to the world.

After all, he is coming back for a church (which is you and me) that is without spot or wrinkle. Ephesians 5:27, KJV states that he might "present it to himself a glorious church, not having spot, or wrinkle, or any such thing; but that it should be holy and without blemish."

What does this really mean to me in the work of the Ministry to the people of God?

He recently the Lord gave me a revelation of the compartments of our heart and mind. In these compartment we categorized events that happen to us on a daily bases. We have a Joyful compartment, Peaceful compartment, Passion compartments, Resentful compartment, rejection compartment and so on. These compartments are developed daily when we do not go before the Lord for a personal inventory. Each daily inventory requires that we put each event in its proper perspective whether it is good or bad, negative, or positive. Each event must be censored by the Holy Spirit which sifts through the impurities and puts it in its proper place in our heart and mind. This is why God's tell us to seek and love him with all our heart and soul. ('And thou shalt love the Lord thy God with all thine heart, and with all thy soul, and with all thy might.' Deuteronomy 6:5, KJV). We are also admonished to, "Keep thy heart with all diligence; for out of it are the issues of life. (Proverbs 4:23, KJV.)

This brings me to the revelation of Tally Space. This is compartments in our heart where keep hurts and issues that others have done against toward us or said against or about us. For instance someone ask you to forgive them for a particular act and every time you think about the act or someone else does something that reminds you of the act. You bring it up to the person, you supposedly have forgiven. It is a space in your heart that you have occupied by a hurtful or abusive situation and you really have not released it to the Lord. So instead we bagger the person that rendered the hurt contiguously with the thing we said we had forgiven them of.

Another instance is we constantly remind our loved ones of what they said and never allow them to change their mind and/or live down what was said at a particular time of having a certain mind set or way of believing. All these behaviorisms are called "tally space" You as the person are keeping a tickler system or a count of wrongs of things you don't approve of. Or a list of wrongs acted out toward you as person.

The sad fact is this space that is taken up by keeping a record of people's wrongs against you is polluting your heart. The major wrong is that this is space you could be filling up with the love of God and His breath. Many times people do not understand why they fill so weighted down with life. It is because we do not allow the Lord to keep our heart. The spirit of the Lord keeps no records of wrong once they are forgiven. Also any act that he avenges is final and everyone knows that it was His doing.

The problem is that tally space shows up in the way we minister to one another. Our attitude toward people and life reflects in our actions toward people. I think it is so awesome that the Lord would pull his disciples aside and say, "you are going to be blessed or happy when you have this attitude."

Most importantly what Jesus is saying to us is that you will not be able to hear me, nor see me revealed in your life if your heart is not pure. The soul that is filled with hate, malice, and polluted does not receive revelation from the Lord. It is impossible. Thus when we are before people ministering to a crowd of millions or standing before one person on your job, you cannot successfully tell them the fresh revelation of the Lord is for their life or yours because your heart is filled with toxic fumes over hurts and unnecessary information.

In order for us to really come before the Lord to receive his will for our Lives we must present ourselves as a child, innocent. We must come as a lamb, as Jesus did, trusting that God, almighty will not harm us, and that he intends the ultimate good for our lives individually and as corporate body.

Tally space is dangerous and must be destroyed from our minds. We must put away and denounce the physical need to retaliate or bring up past wrongs in order to fill our own personal need to get back or correct in a manner that hurts the person and us as an individual. Tally space hinders your relationship with the Lord. Happy is he who has unmixed matters in his heart and presents himself before the Lord innocent that he may receive the pure revelation of God. Daily Prayer is the key to an effective life.

Encounter IV

Life's challenges can either keep us on our in a psychiatric ward or on our knees. I prefer the latter, on my knees. One of the more intense challenges of the Christian life is putting under the desires of our flesh. This means our thought life; our sexual desires; our interaction with people and how we treat them; our need to be accepted and belong. Our need to confirmed and affirmed which has different meanings in each denomination, I do know. However, I am speaking of the need to have those in leadership validate who we are and that we have a calling upon our lives. Those called into leadership in some capacity have this need from the clergy. Many also have the need to be validated by family members in some aspect. It seems to be very stressful to face life's flesh concerns and physical needs without the help of the Holy Spirit. We must in essence exchange a physical or flesh craving for a spiritual groaning. The fruit of the Spirit, found in Galatians when activated in our lives causes us to overcome the fleshly challenges of life through prayer. We must work out our own soul salvation. This requires some work on our part. This requires taking on the assignment of a spiritual groaning. This actually means that we will tread through life's challenges which require praying that sometimes manifest itself through groaning.

In Galatians the Bible states:

'This I say then, Walk in the Spirit, and ye shall not fulfil the lust of the flesh. For the flesh lusteth against the Spirit, and the Spirit against the flesh: and these are contrary the one to the other: so that ye cannot do the things that ye would. But if ye be led of the Spirit, ye are not under the law. Now the works of the flesh are manifest, which are these; Adultery, fornication, uncleanness, lasciviousness, Idolatry, witchcraft, hatred, variance, emulations, wrath, strife, sedation, heresies, Envies, murders, drunkenness, ravelings, and such like: of the which I tell you before, as I have also told you in time past, that they which do such things shall not inherit the kingdom of God. But the fruit of the Spirit is love, joy, peace, longsuffering, gentleness, goodness, faith, Meekness, temperance: against such there is no law. And they that are Christ's have crucified the flesh with the affections and lusts.' (Galatians 5:16-24, KJV).

What does walking in the Spirit mean? It has been explained to us many times and I will not even take on the task of attempting to give a one, two, three, step solution. I believe that walking in the Spirit is an individualized process. What it may take for one person to be delivered from a drug addiction or from an addition to a human being may take something totally different for someone else. However, the one constant is that you must have fellowship with the Lord in order to overcome. Whatever way you choose to have this constant communication, you must find that place of relating to the Spirit of the Lord and keep it as your Survival. It must be a way of life to you.

In order to make an exchange of something physical that you like doing that may or may not be viewed as sin to others, but the Lord has asked you to discard the physical act. One must find a place of intimacy with the Father.

This place of intimacy cannot have any distractions. It must be a place where you spend time with the Father for detoxification and then impartation. You must have time for release and reception. You cannot feel intimated, or ashamed to show yourself to the Lord. It must be a place of full faith and commitment that *Father knows best.*

A lot of times the groan comes from the strong desire to refrain from wrong, however, as you continue to seek the spirit of the Lord and to seek His face on the matter. God will turn the physical craving into a spiritual groan. Spiritual groan is a longing to see the vision of the Lord come forth in its fullness. 'Likewise the Spirit also helpeth our infirmities: for we know not what we should pray for as we ought: but the Spirit itself maketh intercession for us with groanings which cannot be uttered. And he that searcheth the hearts knoweth what is the mind of the Spirit, because he maketh intercession for the saints according to the will of God. (Romans 8:26-27, KJV).

The desire in our hearts to please the Lord causes a transformation in our inner man. This longing to do the will of God captures the heart of the Father and the Jesus begins to intercede on our behalf as well. The Holy Spirit begins to simultaneously sense the breath of the Lord and begins to moan and utter a heavenly language that we dare not understand, or else we could taper with the outcome.

God the Father, El Shaddi, the Almighty One, intends to bring each of His children to their expected end. He longs for us to have the desires of our heart. It would only be right and just for the Creator in us to create through us. The Father desires for us to live happy and full lives that do have challenges but for our ultimate good. In order to manifest the Glory that transforms lives we must allow ourselves time and space to exchange or physical habits for God's Spiritual principals. God's principals always work even for those who don't know him. Relationship with him brings about eternal change. God's principals without relationship bring a means to an end without satisfaction or stability. You will find that you can be married to someone and appear to have a relationship and receive some of the benefits from being a married couple. However, in the end you are not fulfilled because you lack a true relationship and you are just with the person to fill a void or physical need, trying filling all voids with the spirit of the Lord and watch all other relationship mend themselves.

ENCOUNTER V

Picking Up The Mantle

This I know, I know you thought you picked up the mantle back in Chapter I when your water broke. No, No, I am sorry but you were just receiving the mantle, not actually picking it up. To pick up the mantle means operating in and with the anointing designed for your office. The mantle is imparted to you by someone who has gone before you.

A mantle has often been talked about in Christendom, however, I don't know if I have ever fully understood what was meant. I will attempt to give you my understanding through the Holy Spirit. In my studies I have learned that the mantle is a covering that represented a calling to service, protection, sanctification and foremost a covenant relationship with God.

The Merriam-Webster Dictionary describes a mantle as the following:

1. A loose sleeveless garment worn over other clothes.
2. Something that covers, enfolds, or envelopes.
3. A lacy sheath that gives light by incandescence when placed over a flame.
4. The portion of the earth lying between the crust and the core.

The Jewish word for mantle is called tallit, meaning prayer shawl. Many Jewish people still fasten there prayer shawls under their garments, which is called a tallit katan. The tallit kaftan is worn all the time, except when bathing. Then there is the prayer shawl that is worn over the head and shoulders in the temple. Many Christians are beginning to incorporate this powerful cloth into their everyday prayer lives and into corporate worship.

I have incorporated the prayer shawl into my own personal prayer time many years ago. I have found that the intimacy with Father has increased and the anointing upon my life as well. Firsthand experience has made me a believer of the power in the prayer shawl and the residue of the Glory that comes from God above. My first prayer shawl was a gift from my husband- which he had used from many years before passing it on to me. So his mantle and prayer anointing covers me as well when I wear it and when I minister. The most awesome testimony of a mantel being passed is that in the scripture of when Elijah passed the mantle to Elisha. I King 19:19 says, 'So he departed thence, and found Elisha the son of Shaphat, who was plowing with twelve yoke of oxen before him, and he with the twelfth: and Elijah passed by him, and cast his mantle upon him.' (I King 19:19, KJV).

What an honored and powerful moment for Elijah to cast his mantle upon. Mantle can also be interpreted as a calling or ministry. We have heard it said I am passing the mantle down to my son or daughter. Mantles are not only pulpit ministries. Mantles come in all shapes and types of giftings.

Both of my spiritual mothers have a mantle of prayer on their lives, as well as my natural mother. This mantle of prayer was passed on to me by all three of them. Although only one of them, my natural mother passed on to be with the Lord, my two spiritual mothers are still alive and each has imparted their mantle of prayer to me. Blanche Washington is an associate pastor at her local church in Oklahoma City, Oklahoma and a powerful teacher and conference speaker. While my other spiritual mother, Maple Reynolds is the Spiritual advisor to our ministry along with being a loyal member and prayer warrior at her local church in St. Louis, Missouri. Although my mothers have different assignments their God given ministries the foundation is prayer. I truly believe this mantle of prayer along with their other giftings were imparted to me. However, I did have to grow in to some of them. Some of them we in me from birth and just had to be developed. I am still maturing and still teachable. As my husband says about mother Reynolds she has forgotten some of the things we are still trying to learn.

Elijah was one of the greatest prophets. He was from the house of Aaron. Elijah was sometimes spoken of as the prophet of fire and the prophet of resurrecting the dead. Elijah was also the Prophet who prayed earnestly that it might not rain: and it rained not on the earth by the space of three years and six months. I can only imagine the type of glory that was upon the mantle he wore daily. He was a man of great prayer and supplication. As he covered himself daily in the 613 commandments that representative the cloak he wore. I am sure that he was able to command the atmosphere in faith to obey his voice. I believe that Elijah was called the prophet of fire because of the anointing which was on his life. Elijah being a man of great divine insight was so sure of his election of God's chosen to receive his mantle that he passed by him and cast it upon him. Elisha after receiving the mantle did not go right out and build a church or go and get his incorporation papers, and business cards and start a ministry. But look at what the scripture says that he did: 'And he left the oxen, and ran after Elijah, and said, Let me, I pray thee, kiss my father and my mother, and then I will follow thee. And he said unto him, Go back again: for what have I done to thee?' (I Kings 19:20, KJV).

Elisha followed his spiritual father and mentor and what is so awesome is the kinship that happened immediately in the spiritual realm. Elisha is ministering to Elijah. You must be maturing enough to minister to the person set over you without making them less or small. You must be mature enough to not loose respect and moreover know how to minister to the men and women of God effectively. Many times ministering to those called to a people requires only that you listen to their heart. It may require feedback. Most definitely it does not mean carrying their briefcase. Most people of God called with a high calling are people of humility and only require loyalty that only God can give. These people of God are of a different breed and are not Tarrant or task masters. Mentors and spiritual parents will challenge you and guide you. Mantle passers are aware of who the mantle should be given to long before it is casted upon you.

There may be many seasons of walking with the mentor before the mantel is picked up. There will be signs that the mantle has been cast. You will have like mannerisms, like ministries, but not carbon copies, there will be distinct similarities. People will be able to identify who your spiritual parents and mentors are.

I don't want you to think that a mantle can only be received in a church setting. Mantle can be passed from basically any type of profession, or vocation. We see actors that have followed in their parents or mentors footsteps. I see musicians, dancers, artists, and others in the church follow after their mentors. It is an awesome transition to watch. I love to see the changing of the guards. One of my favorites here recently has been the passing per say of the torch of Oprah Winfrey to Tara Banks. Although many may not see the mentorship and the training which was imparted to Tara by Oprah, I find it delightful. Although Oprah still has it going on and is very successful to watch and admire, you can see Tara taking this same anointing into the twenty first century.

Wait Your Turn

It is best to wait your turn and not jump out the starting gate before the gun goes off. It is nothing more embarrassing than to see someone trying to do what they think is right and what they think they know to do and failing miserably before an audience of on lookers. Most of those onlookers are thinking that you should have waited.
Romans 12:7 states, 'Or ministry, let us wait on our ministering: or he that teacheth, on teaching' (Romans 12:7, KJV). The urge to preach or teach is not the anointing or the confirmation to do so. Normally when God really calls you to do a work of any magnitude you will feel very

unqualified. Although you will have the desire and the longing, you will not be hot headed and aggressive. You will be like a lamb going to be slaughtered. Sounds like a Jesus moment to me. It is best to wait until you are almost literally pushed out the gate before you take on the mantle.

Many people in leadership we notice the anointing upon your life long before you do. Many times they we will wait to validate this calling to make sure that you know it for yourself. However, there will be many small confirmations and words of encouragement along the way. Even your friends will notice that you have something great you have to complete in this life time. Do not take words of encouragement and validations as a verbal certificate of license or ordination to start a church. You are only setting yourself up to fail. One must always follow in order to lead. Every great leader has been a follower and a server in his life. Most great leaders remain servers of others for life. I found that my greatest reward is being able to serve others.

Spare yourself some heartache don't step out to soon to do anything without waiting, watching, and witnessing firsthand what happens when you are in charge. Being is charge is being responsible. Being responsible means you catch the blame good or bad. Also you pay the bill. It has been said many times by more prolific and extremely greater people than myself. But it warrants saying again, Count the cost! Count the cost before you say, "oh, I can do that." God anointed you for a position and gives you grace to carry it out. However, when we step out of our lanes and get into personal glory, we mess up every time.

Picking up the mantle requires being a follower. It requires being able to minister to those over and under you. As well as those lateral to you. I love that scripture says that Mary Magdalene and Mary the mother of James ministering to Jesus the Christ in Matthew 27:55. That is so profound yet humbling that these two women were allowed and were counted worthy to minister to Jesus. It was a mantle of servitude in which I am sure was imparted to them from watching Jesus serve others. We must finds ourselves burning with a fire to serve and seek after God's will. However, on the same token we must not let our burning desire cloud our view of the journey. The journey is just as important as the destination. The journey of learning, growing, and maturing is far better than rubies and pearls. No one can take from you what is learned and deposit into your spirit no matter how hard they try.

Pick up the mantle but do it delicately, wisely, and with a teachable spirit.

ENCOUNTER VI

Who Am I?

So many times I had asked myself, who am I? What am I here for? And what in the world is my purpose? Don't act like you have never asked yourself that question. I have leaders approach me today, asking me who do you think I am. What anointing do you think I have? This is not a shameful or embarrassing question to ask. I say you are smart if you are asking, *Who am I?* I think a small majority of today's Christians do not know who God has called them to be. Even after picking up the mantle of a gifting. Many will find themselves still searching to feel a void or answer the question, who am I really?

You will never be happy until you conquer this question and settle it in your mind. You will remain angry with the world until you find out. If you are wondering why you get jealous and envious of others who appear to have what you should have had. It is because you don't know who or more importantly whose you are. It I stopped and took a survey of everyone that picked up this book to read it, and asked do you know who God has called you to be. 90% of people would say I think I know, but I am not totally sure. Okay let me let you off the hook. It is okay!! Now is the time you search your heart and begin to admit you don't know and you need the voice of the Lord to tell you.

'For thou hast possessed my reins: thou hast covered me in my mother's womb. I will praise thee; for I am fearfully and wonderfully made: marvelous are thy works; and that my soul knoweth right well. My substance was not hid from thee, when I was made in secret, and curiously wrought in the lowest parts of the earth. Thine eyes did see my substance, yet being unperfect; and in thy book all my members were written, which in continuance were fashioned, when as yet there was none of them.' (Psalms 139:13-16, KJV).

God is able to tell you who you are. He begins speaking to us in Psalms 139 by saying that in our mother's womb, in the creative state, he has already formed us and covered us. God knew us from the beginning of eternity passed. I think it would be best to ask him the source, from whence you come. If we never learn anything else about ourselves, we must know that God has already spoken and said that we are fearfully and wonderfully made. We could stop right there if we wanted and be grateful and satisfied. We are to be respected and the word wonderful means marvelous, astonishing, and unusually good. Oh my how awesome God is already confirming that each and every one of us are. In our time of studying, my husband and I came across the knowledge, that in Genesis when God said the word "good" it meant His presence. As you read in Genesis, after God made everything, fruit on trees, seed, grass, and fields, beast of the earth, the sea, the fish, and everything that creepeth on the earth. God said it is good, or that is my presence. After God said let us make man in our image, He spoke and said that is very good. Glory to His name. God is saying that my presence is in you. You are my presence, that's who you are, and you are unusually good. You have my presence in a unique way. This should be enough written in the past couple of sentences to cause you to close this book and start dancing around the room.

God the Father is saying this is who you are. You are made in my image, Jesus and I made you after our likeness and He and I are one. You have everything you will ever need to succeed in life. Who we are depends on how much we want to claim the royalty in which we come from. We were all born from a royal kingship and should never live beneath our means. Although life causes us to travel different roads to success we evidently get there staying on the path of righteousness.

You are who God says that you are. People seem to have an untuned crisis going on, more so in the church than in the world. Christians have not come to the conclusion that God is the author and finisher of our faith. We have to become who He has already said that we are. Follow me here; God has already known each of us from the beginning of time. He has settled it in his mind. God will not be changing his thoughts toward you or changing his mind as to who you are? We might but he will not. Even if you were born into a nasty situation and you may not even know who your natural parents are. God knows your DNA and he says that you are his presence. One must seek him to find themselves.

WE have allowed people to label us this or that and I am not going to spend a lot of time talking about this particular issue. However, you may go through a lot of name calling and labeling before you come to the knowing of your

Creator's true vision of who you really are. God will not keep it a secret from you. The issue is that we have many voices and many traditions that shape our fate. Some of us have been groomed from birth to carry a torch that was never meant to be. What am I saying? Do not be hard or yourself if you have labeled yourself or allowed others to label you as having a certain gifting, talents, or titles. Chalk it all up as experience. Now we get to look back and see what we are not. It's all good. Yes that's right, it is all God's presence molding and shaping our eternal futures.

There have been many wonderful books written by very prolific writers, such as Dr. Myles Munroe, John Maxwell, and many others talking about purpose and leadership. I will not attempt to devise your purpose because they have done such a spectacular job of doing so. I would admonish you to purchase their work and began pen pointing who you are.

Remember God say's that you are his Presence.

ENCOUNTER VII

In His Presence

In His presence is fullness of joy and pleasure ever more this is in Psalms 16:11. Oh how true I have found this passage of scripture to be. It comes to life right off the pages of the bible. The full scripture reads thus so:

'Thou wilt shew me the path of life: in thy presence is fullness of joy; at thy right hand there are pleasures for evermore.' (Psalms 16:11, KJV).

The Greater Yes is to say yes to his presence, saying yes to the call of the Lord to come and talk with him is the greatest yes. The benefits of communicating outweigh anything else in life. God starts out with the promise that he will show you the path of life. If we will come to Him and spend time, He will show us every and any thing we need to know. So many times we substitute other tasks, and minimal doings for God's presence. We would rather be doing Godly stuff; some of us even do religious stuff thinking it is spending time with God. What do I mean we do things that are traditional and habits? For instance we get up go to church every week, and throughout the week. This is a doing and a happening. It is an act of doing something we feel is pleasing to God and we count it as time spent with him personally. Church is good and fellowship one with another is good. And corporate worship is awesome and powerful. However, all of this does not take the place of spending alone time with God. Sometimes we even watch a good preacher on TV or catch a good Christian movie or do a good deed and count this as time spent with God. It is time spent for Him and on His behalf doing his will. It cannot be counted as significant quality time.

In order to receive an impartation or download from eternity, you must spend quality alone time with God. You must stay long enough to get an impartation and to conceive what the Spirit of the Lord wants to birth in you. We have mistaken prayer for a give me, bless me time, and have not taken the time sometimes to even say hello to God. Acknowledging that God is Lord of our lives is a key to learning who you are and what you must do in this life.

It is so funny to me sometimes that God begins to show me myself and I thought I knew myself, Not. He knew me better and first. Beginning to know God intimately is the Key to success. It is in His presence that he reveals secrets and mysteries. God begins to unravel events, situations, and circumstances when we take the time to inquire of him about the challenges we face in day to day life. There is nothing that happens under or above the sun that God does not know about.

I admonish you to say yes to the call of God to prayer. Prayer is a legal and lethal weapon in the earth and in the heavenliness. God is waiting to hear your voice triumph through the air waves. So many times God only has opportunity to hear the cry of distress. God seldom gets to hear a cry of worship or a cry of admiration. I would love to see the believers begin to turn to God not for help but for humility. I would love to see people hearts melt by the mention of the name of Jesus. The Jews reverence the name of God so, that they would not even say it. He is called Hashem meaning the Name. He is called YHVH. His name is not to spelled, it is so Holy. If we would begin to reverence our Father God in love and admiration, His very presence would overtake us. This may sound fearful to some. However, when the spirit of the Lord overtakes you, you begin to know all things. He brings all truth with him. You no longer have to wonder about situations, the answer in wisdom is given immediately. God all-knowing power is able to bring peace to any situation.

We must continue to seek his face like never before for counsel. I know this has been said before seek his face. The Spirit of the Lord gave me a revelation of seeking His face back in June of 2008. The Spirit said to me that seeking my face means to seek my hearing, seek my sight and vision. To seek my discernment and speak what I say out of your mouth. Oh my, how blessed and overcome I was in that moment in my prayer room when the Spirit of the Lord said this to me. Your physical face is liken unto my spiritual face. You have eyes, ears, nose, and mouth. I don't but I can talk to you in what you know in your realm. Oh my. I wanted it God face. If I can know what he knows and say what he says I will have it made.

Seek his Presence this is the GREATER YES, not answering the call to minister, or being given a title. Answering the call to come when he calls you unto himself is the sacrificial, yet beneficial Yes.

'But without faith it is impossible to please him: for he that cometh to God must believe that he is, and that he is a rewarder of them that diligently seek him.' (Hebrew 11:6, KJV).

ENCOUNTER VIII

Walking with God

This Walking with God is a loyal commitment you must establish within yourself before you try and serve others. As we commitment to a work or a body of people, we must find ourselves committed to the call of God. Rather we commitment a job or a people and often we are let down.

Walking with God will manifest some ups and downs. Also casualties, upsets, setups, and many victories. Genesis 5:23-24 states, 'And all the days of Enoch were three hundred sixty and five years: And Enoch walked with God: and he was not; for God took him.' (Genesis 5:23-24 KJV).

While writing this book, the Spirit of the Lord has imparted to me revelation upon revelation; one of which I would like to submit to you about Enoch. I have read the above passage of scripture before and assumed that Enoch died and ascended into eternity with God, never to be seen by mankind again. However, God began to reveal to me that as you seek the Lord on a daily bases, as Enoch did 365 days – which makes up a year for us. You will cease to exist, meaning the way you think and act is no more. You become transformed into the total likeness of God himself. The word says and Enoch was not. He did not think like himself, talk like himself, behave like himself. But all things were like God and then God had taken him or apprehended him, caught him up to be with him. I believe that Enoch continued to minister in the earth but that he was so much like God that his existence was no more and family and friends were unable to recognize that it was Enoch.

This would be so awesome that we take on the traits of God our Father in Prayer and that we walk with Him in such a manner every day that the world would began to see truly the city that sits on a hill.

'Ye are the light of the world. A city that is set on a hill cannot be hid.' (Matthew 5:14, KJV).

We that are called by God should be a light for the whole world to see. We should have all the answers to life's problems through the Holy Spirit. People should be healed by our loving-kindness. The world should find hope in our eyes and in our words comfort should be found.

Walking with God will not always be sunny days but it will be exciting. God will give you peace that surpasses all understanding in all things. Walking with God determines the Glory upon your life. In other words the amount of authority and power you exhibit. Walking with God separates the wannabes from the JUST IS. Walking with God makes the difference. We must fellowship to receive the Glory that comes after we have been anointed to do a work.

I guarantee you, if you walk with God, he will make known to you your calling in this life and He will finish that which he started. Blessings to you.

(Write your name in the blanks)

My Prayer for you, as you seek God about the Ministry He has given you to manage in the Earth:

I thank you, Father God, that _____ has been called as your vessel in the earth. You have declared them worthy and fit to run the race in which you have given them. You have solidified, and validated the ministry in which you have made them responsible for. Lord God, Elohim, Creator, you have created _____ in your likeness, and in your character, and strength. Through daily prayer and fellowship, you will equip them for the task before. We seal this prayer with a kiss, the kiss of the Holy Spirit. This prayer shall not return void, it shall, and has accomplished what it was sent to do. In the name of Yeshua, Our Messiah, Jesus the Christ. And it is So!